T0057926

Also by Frederick Seidel

THE COSMOS TRILOGY

BARBADOS

AREA CODE 212

LIFE ON EARTH

THE COSMOS POEMS

GOING FAST

MY TOKYO

THESE DAYS

POEMS, 1959–1979

SUNRISE

FINAL SOLUTIONS

OOGA-BOOGA

Ooga-Booga

FREDERICK SEIDEL

FARRAR, STRAUS AND GIROUX
NEW YORK

Farrar, Straus and Giroux
18 West 18th Street, New York 10011

Copyright © 2006 by Frederick Seidel
All rights reserved

Printed in the United States of America
Published in 2006 by Farrar, Straus and Giroux
First paperback edition, 2007

The Library of Congress has cataloged the
hardcover edition as follows:
Seidel, Frederick, 1936–
    Ooga-booga / Frederick Seidel.— 1st ed.
    p.   cm.
    ISBN-13: 978-0-374-22655-8 (alk. paper)
    ISBN-10: 0-374-22655-5 (alk. paper)
    I. Title.

PS3569.E5 O58 2006
811'.54—dc22

                                        2006002698

Paperback ISBN-13: 978-0-374-53097-6
Paperback ISBN-10: 0-374-53097-1

Designed by Peter A. Andersen

www.fsgbooks.com

TO FELICITY AND SAM

CONTENTS

OOGA-BOOGA

KILL POEM

Huntsman indeed is gone from Savile Row,
And Mr. Hall, the head cutter.
The red hunt coat Hall cut for me was utter
Red melton cloth thick as a carpet, cut just so.
One time I wore it riding my red Ducati racer—what a show!—
Matched exotics like a pair of lovely red egrets.
London once seemed the epitome of no regrets
And the old excellence one used to know
Of the chased-down fox bleeding its stink across the snow.

We follow blindly, clad in coats of pink,
A beast whose nature is to run and stink.
I am civilized in my pink but
Civilized is about having stuff.
The red coats are called "pinks." Too much is almost enough.
No one knows why they are. I parade in the air
With my stuff and watch the disappearing scut
Of a deer. I am civilized but
Civilized life is actually about too much.

I parade in the air
And wait for the New Year
That then will, then will disappear.
I am trying not to care.
I am not able not to.
A short erect tail
Winks across the winter field.
All will be revealed.
I am in a winter field.

They really are everywhere.
They crawl around in one's intimate hair.
They spread disease and despair.
They rape and pillage
In the middle of Sag Harbor Village.
They ferry Lyme disease.
The hunters' guns bring them to their knees.
In Paris I used to call the Sri Lankan servants "Shrees."
I am not able not to.

Winter, spring, Baghdad, fall,
Venery is written all
Over me like a rash,
Hair and the gash,
But also the Lehrer *NewsHour* and a wood fire and Bach.
A short erect tail
Winks across the killing field.
All will be revealed.
I am in a killing field.

I remember the *chasse à courre* in the forest in the Cher.
I remember the English thoroughbreds ridden by the frogs.
I remember the weeping stag cornered by the dogs.
The stag at bay in the pond literally shed a tear.
A hunt servant in a tricorn hat waded out to cut its throat.
Nelson Aldrich on his horse vomited watching this.
The huntsman's heraldic horn sounded the *hallali*.
The tune that cuts off the head. *L'hallali!*
Back to the château to drink the blood. *L'hallali!*

I am in Paris being introduced at Billy's,
1960, Avenue Paul-Valéry.
One of her beautiful imported English Lillys or Millys
Is walking around on her knees.
It is rather like that line of Paul Valéry's.
Now get down on all fours, please.
We are ministers of state and then there is me chez Billy.
Deer garter-belt across our field of vision
And stand there waiting for our decision.

Our only decision was how to cook the venison.
I am civilized but
I see the silence
And write the words for the thought-balloon.
When the woods are the color of a macaroon,
Deer, death is near.
I write about its looks in my books.
I write disappearing scut.
I write rut.

The title is *Kill Poetry*,
And in the book poetry kills.
In the poem the stag at bay weeps, literally.
Kill poetry is the *hallali* on Avenue Paul-Valéry.
Get rid of poetry. Kill poetry.
Label on a vial of pills. Warning: Kill kill kill kills.
Its title is *Kill Poem*,
From the *Book of Kills*.
The antlered heads are mounted weeping all around the walls.

John F. Kennedy is mounted weeping on the wall.
His weeping brother Robert weeps nearby.
Martin Luther King, at bay in Memphis, exhausted, starts to cry.
His antlered head is mounted weeping on the wall.
Too much is almost enough, for crying out loud!
Bobby Kennedy announces to a nighttime crowd
That King has died, and then quotes Aeschylus, and then is killed.
Kill kill kill kills, appalls,
The American trophies covered in tears that deck the American halls.

FROM NIJINSKY'S DIARY

And when the doctor told me that I could have died.
And when I climbed up from the subway to the day outside.
White summer clouds were boiling in the trees.
I felt like falling to my knees.
Stand clear of the closing doors, please! Stand clear of the closing doors, please!

And when the camel knelt to let me mount it.
Winged angels knelt in silhouette
To worship at the altar made of blue
That the sun was fastened to.
It all came down to you. It all comes down to you.

In New York City "kneeling" buses kneel for the disabled.
My camel kneels. We fly into the desert.
I flee in terror to my tranquilizer the Sahara.
I stroll slowly down sweet Broadway.
It is as you say. We are here to pray.

VIOLIN

I often go to bed with a book
And immediately turn out the light.
I wake in the morning and brush and dress and go to the desk and write.
I always put my arm in the right sleeve before I slip into the left.
I always put on my left shoe first and then I put on the right.

I happen right now
To be walking the dogs in the dangerous park at night,
Which is dangerous, which I do not like,
But I am delighted, my dog walk is a delight.
I am right-handed but mostly I am not thinking.

(CHORUS)
A man can go to sleep one night and never wake up that he knows of.
A man can walk down a Baghdad street and never walk another drop.
A man can be at his publisher's and drop dead on the way to the men's room.
A poet can develop frontotemporal dementia.
A flavorful man can, and then he is not.

The call girls who came to our separate rooms were actually lovely.
Weren't they shocked that their customers were so illegally young?
Mine gently asked me what I wanted to do. Sin is Behovely.
Just then the phone rang—
Her friend checking if she was safe with the young Rambo, Rimbaud.

I am pursuing you, life, to the ends of the earth across a Sahara of
     tablecloth.
I look around the restaurant for breath.
I stuff my ears to sail past the siren song of the rocks.
The violin of your eyes
Is listening gently.

NECTAR

A rapist's kisses tear the leaves off.
Aiuto!
The world looks so white on the white pillow.
I think I know you. I don't think so.

Winter is wearing summer but it wants to undress for you, Fred.
Oh my God. Takes off the lovely summer frock
And lies down on the bed naked
Freezing white, so we can make death.

Joel and I were having lunch at Fred's,
The restaurant on the ninth floor of Barneys
Where Joel likes to eat when he is in New York,
Who had just landed, and when I ask him what astonishment

He is carrying around with him this time,
He takes out of his jacket pocket
A beige *pochette*,
And out pops a stupefying diamond ring I know from Paris.

It opens its big eye.
It went nonstop to Florida in his pocket on the plane.
Now returns with a stop in Manhattan to the JAR safe, Place Vendôme.
I have to try it on.

It is incredible what travels
Unprotected in that pocket through the time zones.
I look down at my finger
And field-trip an alternate universe.

Don't I know you? I don't think so. It is not for sale.
Diane von Furstenberg in those sweet bygone days
Got it in her head I had to meet her friend
The jeweler to the stars.

Two hummingbirds hummed across the Pont des Arts,
And through the *cour du Louvre*, to Joel's JAR.
At her old apartment at 12, Rue de Seine,
We lived like hummingbirds on nectar and oxygen.

ON BEING DEBONAIR

Shirts wear themselves out being worn.
Suits fit perfectly,
But a man does
Decades of push-ups and no longer fits.
I take myself out to dinner.
It is a joy to sit alone
Without a book.
I use myself up being fine while I dine.
I am a result of the concierge at the Carlyle.
I order a bottle of Bordeaux.
I am a boulevard of elegance
In my well-known restaurants.

The moon comes over to my table.
Everything about her is typical.
I like the way she speaks to me.
Everything about me is bespoke.
You are not
Known, and you are not no one.
I remember you from before.
Sometimes I don't go out till the end of the day.
I simply forget till
I rush out, afraid the day will end.
Every sidewalk tree is desperate
For someone.

The desert at this time of year
Is troops in desert camouflage.
Bring in the unmanned drones.
I dine with my Carlyle smile.
She tells me spring will come.
The moon stops by my table
To tell me.
I will cut your heart out
And drink the rubies and eat the coral.
I like the female for its coral.
I go to Carnegie Hall
To make her open her mouth onstage and scream.

HOMAGE TO PESSOA

I once loved,
I thought I would be loved,
But I wasn't loved.
I wasn't loved for the only reason that matters—
It was not to be.
I unbuttoned my white gloves and stripped each off.
I set aside my gold-knobbed cane.
I picked up this pen . . .
And thought how many other men
Had smelled the rose in the bud vase
And lifted a fountain pen,
And lifted a mountain . . .
And put the shotgun in their mouth,
And noticed that their hunting dog was pointing.

FOR HOLLY ANDERSEN

What could be more pleasant than talking about people dying,
And doctors really trying,
On a winter afternoon
At the Carlyle Hotel, in our cocoon?
We also will be dying one day soon.

Dr. Holly Andersen has a vodka cosmopolitan,
And has another, and becomes positively Neapolitan,
The moon warbling a song about the sun,
Sitting on a sofa at the Carlyle,
Staying stylishly alive for a while.

Her spirited loveliness
Does cause some distress.
She makes my urbanity undress.
I present symptoms that express
An underlying happiness in the face of the beautiful emptiness.

She lost a very sick patient she especially cared about.
The man died on the table. It wasn't a matter of feeling any guilt or doubt.
Something about a doctor who can cure, or anyway try,
But can also cry,
Is some sort of ultimate lullaby, and lie.

FOG

I spend most of my time not dying.
That's what living is for.
I climb on a motorcycle.
I climb on a cloud and rain.
I climb on a woman I love.
I repeat my themes.

Here I am in Bologna again.
Here I go again.
Here I go again, getting happier and happier.
I climb on a log
Torpedoing toward the falls.
Basically, it sticks out of me.

At the factory,
The racer being made for me
Is not ready, but is getting deadly.
I am here to see it being born.
It is snowing in Milan, the TV says.
They close one airport, then both.

The Lord is my shepherd and the Director of Superbike Racing.
He buzzes me through three layers of security
To the innermost secret sanctum of the racing department
Where I will breathe my last.
Trains are delayed.
The Florence sky is falling snow.

Tonight Bologna is fog.
This afternoon, there it was,
With all the mechanics who are making it around it.
It stood on a sort of altar.
I stood in a sort of fog,
Taking digital photographs of my death.

A RED FLOWER

The poet stands on blue-veined legs, waiting for his birthday to be over.
He dangles from a Muse who works the wires
That make a puppet move in lifelike ways onstage.
Happy birthday to a *semper paratus* penis!
His tiny Cartier wristwatch trumpets it!
He dares to wear a tiny thing that French and feminine.
Nose tilted up, arrogance, blue eyes.
He can smell the ocean this far inland.

We are in France. We are in Italy. We are in England. We are in heaven.
Lightning with a noose around its neck, feet on a cloud,
Drops into space, feet kicking, neck broken.
The parachute pops open . . . a red flower:
Plus ne suis ce que j'ai été,
Et plus ne saurais jamais l'être.
Mon beau printemps et mon été
Ont fait le saut par la fenêtre.

DICK AND FRED

His dick is ticking . . .
Tick tick tick tick . . .
The bomb looks for blonde.
It smiles like a dog.

Werner Muensterberger liked to say to his patients
A stiff prick has no conscience . . .
Tick tick tick tick . . .
Fred Astaire in a tuxedo is doing a blind man with a white cane.

He is looking for blonde.
He looks for brunette.
He licks to play golf.
A bomb is blind.

There was a king.
His name was King Wow.
Anyhow,
In the kingdom of Ebola,

It was on his mind
Constantly. Be kind,
King, be a kind king.
The oceans rose.

About the queen his mother, Gertrude.
Shit with a cunt!
The prince was blunt.
Shit with a cunt.

Cunt with a dick!
Judith slew Holofernes.
Cut his head off.
Slew slime.

Cunt with a dick
Cut the monster's head off.
Holofernes' startled head farts blood
And falls off.

Man delights not me; no, nor woman neither.
Viagra has caused blindness
In thirty-eight impotent men
Who paid for their erections with their eyes.

One man in his eighties took the pill
For the first time and went blind
When his penis started to rise
For the first time in years.

Imagine his double surprise!
The joyous, fastidious, perfectionist
Fred Astaire flies!
Astaire,

Debonair,
Tap-dances the monomania and mania
Of Napoleon Bonaparte's tiny penis, the up.
Fred flies, fappingly, bappingly,

Tick-tick-tick-tick-tappingly,
That athletic nonchalance that Fred Astaire defined.
A penis in a tuxedo is flying all over the place
With the white cane of the blind!

Fred is dancing on a tilting dance floor on the ocean floor
In a sunken ocean liner
In 1934—lighter than air!—Fred Astaire!—
In the depths of the Great Depression.

White people froze the world markets to a great whiteness.
The world will end tomorrow.
They walk around like penguins in their tuxedos.
The planet is frozen.

NEW YEAR'S DAY, 2004

It used to be called the Mayfair.
Leonardo Mondadori used to stay there.
The lobby was the bar.
Fancy Italians were on display.
They sat in the lobby for years.
They seduced from the lavish armchairs.
They told their driver and car to be waiting outside
On their European cell phones.

I was a Traveller then upon the moor.
I walked directly through and down the three stairs.
Their women were theirs.
The Milanese women wore couture.
They smoked cigarettes and smiled and did not blink.
They were going to eat at Le Cirque.
Who could have been kinder than Leonardo?
It was a long time ago.

THE ITALIAN GIRL

Monsoon is over but it's raining.
The rain keeps coming down. It gets you down. It's draining.
The sticky heat in Singapore is really not that entertaining.
The boutique hotel air-conditioning is aquaplaning.
The rain stops just inside the door and the fashion show goes on.

So they board the little tram at the zoo to do the "Night Safari"
To experience wild animals who are separate but equal.
The Chinese tour-guide puts her finger to her lips: "Let us be quiet."
They hear the silence roar
In humid Singapore.

Nobody has hair like this Italian girl, in this humidity!
She came three days ago to do the fashion show.
She hadn't cut her mane in weeks.
She loves the hippos bathing in the perspiring water.
Her curls are African lions exploding from a thicket.

THE BIG GOLCONDA DIAMOND

The Master Jeweler Joel Rosenthal, of the Bronx and Harvard,
Is Joel Arthur Rosenthal of JAR, Place Vendôme.
The greatest jeweler of our time
Has brought to Florida from his safe
A big Golconda diamond that is matchless,
So purely truthful it is not for sale, Joel's favorite, his Cordelia.
His mother in Florida can keep it
If she wants, and she doesn't want.
Love is mounted on a fragile platinum wire
To make a ring not really suitable for daily wear.

I wore the bonfire on a wire, on loan from Joel,
One sparkling morning long ago in Paris.
I followed it on my hand across the Pont des Arts
Like Shakespeare in a trance starting the sonnet sequence.

WHAT ARE MOVIES FOR?

Razzle-dazzle on the surface, wobbled-Jell-O sunlight,
A goddess and her buttocks walk across a bridge,
Electrocute the dazed, people can't believe it's her.
The Seine sends waves toward Notre-Dame.
She's here without an entourage, she stands there all alone.
A woman standing at the rail is jumping in broad daylight
From the Pont des Arts, and thinks of jumping.
Her flames almost reach the Institut de France.
It bursts into flame.
A tenement suddenly collapsing vomits fireworks.
A soda jerk pulls the lever
That squirts the soda
That makes an old-time ice cream soda of flames.
A Pullman porter turns down the stateroom bed, white crisp sheets,
Clean as ice,
The clickety-click American night outside,
A Thousand and One Nights inside the star's head.
Miles of antebellum slums, old St. Louis hot at night,
Rows of antebellum houses of white trash in the Southern moonlight:
Developers took advantage of Title 1 funds to pulverize
The picturesque so they could put up miles of projects,
The largest undertaking of its kind in the United States,
So poorly constructed that a few years later
The whole hideous thing would have to be leveled.
I feel such joy.
I stare at sparkles. I don't care.

The carbonated bubbled bloodstream gushes out.
Kiss me here. *Ouf!* Kiss me there.
The crocodile of joy lifts the nostrils of his snout.
His eyes of joy stare at her eyes.
I want to eat between your eyes and hear your cries.
I don't care who lives or dies.
I am the crocodile of joy, who never lies.

THE OWL YOU HEARD

The owl you heard hooting
In the middle of the night wasn't me.
It was an owl.
Or maybe you were
So asleep you didn't even hear it.
The sprinklers on their timer, programmed to come on
At such a strangely late hour in life
For watering a garden,
Refreshed your sleep four thousand miles away by
Hissing sweetly,
Deepening the smell of green in Eden.
You heard the summer chirr of insects.
You heard a sky of stars.
You didn't know it, fast asleep at dawn in Paris.
You didn't hear a thing.
You heard me calling.
I am no longer human.

E-MAIL FROM AN OWL

The irrigation system wants it to be known it *irrigates*
The garden,
It doesn't water it.
It is a stickler about this!
Watering is something done by hand.
Automated catering naturally
Does a better job than a hand with a watering can can.
Devised in Israel to irrigate their orange groves,
It gives life everywhere in the desert of life it goes.
It drips water to the chosen, one zone at a time.
Drip us this day our daily bread, or, rather, this night,
Since a drop on a leaf in direct sunlight can make
A magnifying glass that burns an innocent at the stake.
The sprinkler system hisses kisses on a timer
Under an exophthalmic sky of stars.
Tonight my voice will stare at you forever.
I click on Send,
And send you this perfumed magic hour.

WHITE BUTTERFLIES

I

Clematis paniculata sweetens one side of Howard Street.
White butterflies in pairs flutter over the white flowers.
In white kimonos, giggling and whispering,
The butterflies titter and flutter their silk fans,
End-of-summer cabbage butterflies, in white pairs.
Sweet autumn clematis feeds these delicate souls perfume.
I remember how we met, how shyly.

II

Four months of drought on the East End ends.
Ten thousand windshield wipers wiping the tears away.
The back roads are black.
The ocean runs around barking under the delicious rain, so happy.
Traditional household cleaners polish the Imperial palace floors
Of heaven spotless. THUNDER. Cleanliness and order
Bring universal freshness and good sense to the Empire. LIGHTNING.

III

I have never had a serious thought in my life on Gibson Lane.
A man turning into cremains is standing on the beach.
I used to walk my dog along the beach.
This afternoon I had to put him down.
Jimmy my boy, my sweetyboy, my Jimmy.
It is night, and outside the house, at eleven o'clock,
The lawn sprinklers come on in the rain.

THE CASTLE IN THE MOUNTAINS

I brought a stomach flu with me on the train.
I spent the night curled up in pain,
Agonizingly cold and rather miserable.
I went out for a walk earlier today:
Snow started falling
Like big cotton balls this morning
And the park looks beautiful.
I will try to eat tonight: steamed cauliflower.
You would love it here.
It is still quite nice somehow.

You would like the Emperor.
Some days the joy is overpowering.
The last time I was here,
He told a story.
It was Christmas.
Snow kept falling.
The Emperor held his hand up for silence and began.
His fingernails have perfect moons, which is quite rare.
You hardly see it anymore, I wonder why.

The Emperor began:
"Prehistoric insects were
Flying around brainless
To add more glory to the infant Earth.
Instead of horrible they were huge and beautiful,
And, being angels, were invincible.
Say the Name, and the angel begging with its hand out would
Instantly expand upward
To be as tall as the building . . ."

The ruthless raw odor of filth in an enclosed space,
And the slime tentacles with religious suckers,
And the four heads on one neck like the four heads carved on
      Mt. Rushmore,
Hold out a single hand.

Hold out your hand.
Take my hand.

A FRESH STICK OF CHEWING GUM

A pink stick of gum unwrapped from the foil,
That you hold between your fingers on the way home from dance class,
And you look at its pink. But you know what.
I like your brain. Your pink. It's sweet.

My brain is the wrinkles of the ocean on a ball of tar
Instead of being sweet pink like yours.
It could be the nicotine. It could be the Johnnie Walker Black.
Mine thought too many cigarettes for too many years.

My brain is the size of the largest living thing, *mais oui*, a blue whale,
Blue instead of pink like yours.
It's what I've done
To make it huge that made it huge.

The violent sweetness in the air is the pink rain
Which continues achingly almost to fall.
This is the closest it has come.
This can't go on.

Twenty-six years old is not childhood.
You are not trying to stop smoking.
You smoke and drink
And *still* it is pink.

The answer is you can drink and smoke
Too much at twenty-six,
And stink of cigarettes,
And stand outside on the sidewalk outside the bar to have a cigarette,

As the law now requires, and it is paradise,
And be the most beautiful girl in the world,
And be moral,
And vibrate into blank.

DANTE'S BEATRICE

I ride a racer to erase her.
Bent over like a hunchback.
Racing leathers now include a hump
That protects the poet's spine and neck.
I wring the thing out, two hundred miles an hour.
I am a mink on a mink ranch determined not
To die inside its valuable fur, inside my racesuit.

I bought the racer
To replace her.
It became my slave and I its.
All it lacked was tits.
All it lacked
Between its wheels was hair.
I don't care.
We do it anyway.

The starter-caddy spins its raving little wheel
Against the Superbike's elevated fat black
Rear soft-compound tire.
Remember: *racer*—
Down for second gear instead of up!
Release the clutch—the engine fires.
I am off for my warm-up lap on a factory racer
Because I can't face her.

I ride my racer to erase her.
I ride in armor to
Three hundred nineteen kilometers an hour.
I am a mink on a mink ranch about
To die inside its valuable fur,
Inside my leathers.
She scoops me out to make a coat for her.
She buttons up a me of soft warm blur.

Is this the face that launched
A thousand slave ships?
The world is just outstanding.
My slavery never wavers.
I use the word "slavers"
To mean both "drools"
And, changing the pronunciation, "trades in slaves."
I consider myself most of these.

Mark Peploe and I used to sit around
Cafés in Florence grading
Muses' noses.
Hers hooks like Gauguin's,
His silent huge hooked hawk prow.
I am the cactus. You are the hyena.
I am the crash, you the fireball of Jet-A . . .
Only to turn catastrophe into dawn.

BOLOGNA

My own poetry I find incomprehensible.
Actually, I have no one.
Everything in art is couplets.
Mine don't rhyme.

Everything in the heart, you meant to say.
As if I ever meant to say anything.
Don't get me wrong.
I do without.

I find the poetry I write incomprehensible,
But at least I understand it.
It opens the marble
And the uniforms of the lobby staff

Behind the doorman at 834 Fifth.
Each elevator opens
On one apartment to a floor.
The elevator opened

To the page.
The elevator opened on the little vestibule
On the verge of something.
I hope I have. I hope I don't.

The vagina-eyed Modigliani nude
Made me lewd.
I waited for my friend to descend
The inner staircase of the duplex.

Keyword: house key.
You need a danger to be safe in.
Except in the African bush where you don't,
You do.

The doorway to my childhood
Was the daytime doorman.
An enormously black giant wore an outfit
With silver piping.

He wore a visored cap
With a high Gestapo peak
On his impenetrably black marble.
Waits out there in the sun to open the car door.

My noble Negro statue's name was Heinz,
My calmly grand George Washington.
You'll find me
At my beloved Hotel Baglioni

In Bologna
Still using the word Negro.
I need a danger to be safe in,
In room 221.

George Washington was calmly kind.
The defender of my building was George Washington
With a Nazi name
In World War II St. Louis.

Heinz stood in the terrible sun after
The Middle Passage in his nearly Nazi uniform.
He was my Master Race White Knight.
I was his white minnow.

The sun roars gloriously hot today.
Piazza Santo Stefano might as well be Brazzaville.
The humidity is a divinity.
Huck is happy on the raft in the divinity!

They show movies at night on an outdoor screen
In the steam in Piazza Maggiore.
I'm about to take a taxi
To Ducati

And see Claudio Domenicali, and see Paolo Ciabatti,
To discuss the motorcycle being made for me.
One of the eight factory Superbike racers
Ducati Corse will make for the year,

Completely by hand, will be mine.
I want to run racing slicks
On the street for the look,
Their powerful fat smooth black shine.

I need them
To go nowhere fast and get there.
I need to begin to
Write the poem of Colored Only.

When Heinz took my little hand in his,
Into the little vestibule on the verge
Of learning to ride a bicycle,
I began *Bologna*.

Federico Minoli of Bologna presides
In an unair-conditioned apartment fabulously
Looking out on the seven churches
In Piazza Santo Stefano, in the town center.

The little piazza opens
A little vestibule on the verge of something.
The incredible staircase to his place opens
On seven churches at the top.

The only problem is the bongo drums at night.
Ducati's president and CEO is the intelligent Federico.
Late tonight I will run into him and his wife
At Cesarina, in the brown medieval

Piazza, a restaurant Morandi
Used to lunch at,
Bologna's saintly pure painter of stillness.
I will sit outside in the noisy heat and eat.

RACER

For Paolo Ciabatti

I spend most of my time not dying.
That's what living is for.
I climb on a motorcycle.
I climb on a cloud and rain.
I climb on a woman I love.
I repeat my themes.

Here I am in Bologna again.
Here I go again.
Here I go again, getting happier and happier.
I climb on a log
Torpedoing toward the falls.
Basically, it sticks out of me.

The F-16s take off in a deafening flock,
Shattering the runway at the airbase at Cervia.
They roar across horizontally
And suddenly go straight up,
And then they lean backwards and level off
And are gone till lunchtime and surprisingly wine.

So funny to see the Top Guns out of their G suits get so Italian
In front of the fire crackling in the fireplace.
Toasts are drunk to their guests, much use of hands.
They are crazy about motorcycles
In the officers' mess of the 23rd Squadron.
Over a period of time, one plane in ten is lost.

I hear the man with the silent Chow Chow
Tooting his saxophone
Down in the street, Via dell' Indipendenza, Independence Street.
The dog chats with no one.
The man chats with everyone
With gusto and delight, and accepts contributions.

At the factory,
The racer being made for me
Is not ready, but is getting deadly.
I am here to see it being born.
It is snowing in Milan, the TV says.
They close one airport, then both.

The Lord is my shepherd and the Director of Superbike Racing.
He buzzes me through three layers of security
To the innermost secret sanctum of the racing department.
I enter the adytum.
Trains are delayed.
The Florence sky is falling snow.

The man with the silent Chow Chow
Is tooting in the street
Below my room at the Hotel Baglioni—the Bag in Bo—
My marble home away from home, room 221.
He buzzes me through three layers of security,
Poetry, Politics, Medicine, into the adytum.

Tonight Bologna is fog.
This afternoon, there it was,
With all the mechanics who are making it around it.
It stood on a sort of altar.
I stood in a sort of fog,
Taking digital photographs of my death.

AT A FACTORY IN ITALY

The Man of La Mamma is a tenor as brave as a lion.
Everything is also its towering opposite.
Butch heterosexuals in Italy spend lavishly on fragrances.
The in thing was to shave your head, the skinhead look.
Guys spend more on beauty products here
Than in any other country in the world.
Everyone is also a boss.

The English executive assistant to the Italian CEO stays blondly exuberant
When sales to America plummet, when the dollar is weak.
Her name is Alice Coleridge. Her phone rings nonstop. *Pronto, sono
    Aleecheh!*
The world at the other end of the phone is a charging rhinoceros.
A descendant of Samuel Taylor Coleridge speaks Italian to the rhinoceros.
Poetry has power, as against the men and women actually making things
On the assembly line on the ground floor.

Someone had the brilliant idea of using
Factory workers in the ads,
And using a fashion photographer to add elegance and surprise.
They found an incredible face on the ground floor
With a nose to die for, and paid her to straddle
A motorcycle her assembly line had made and pose in profile.
So what did the Italian nose do? She ran with the money to get a nose job.

FRANCE FOR BOYS

There wasn't anyone to thank.
Two hours from Paris in a field.
The car was burning in a ditch.
Of course, the young star of the movie can't be killed off so early.

He felt he had to get off the train when he saw the station
     sign CHARLEVILLE—
Without knowing why—but something had happened there.
Rimbaud explodes with too good,
With the terrible happiness of light.

He was driving fast through
The smell of France, the French trees
Lining the roads with metronomic to stroboscopic
Bringing-on-a-stroke whacks of joyous light.

They were drunk. It had rained.
Going around the Place de la Concorde too fast
On slippery cobbles, and it happened.
Three spill off the motorcycle, two into a paddy wagon.

Eeehaw, Eeehaw, a midsummer night's dream
Down the boulevard along the Seine.
The most beautiful American girl in France
Has just stepped out of a swimming pool, even in a police van.

Eeehaw, Eeehaw,
In a Black Maria taking them to a hospital.
The beautiful apparently thought the donkey she had just met was dying,
And on the spot fell in love.

The wife of the American Ambassador to France
Took her son and his roommate to Sunday lunch
At a three-star restaurant some distance from Paris.
The chauffeur drove for hours to get to the sacred place.

The roommate proudly wore the new white linen suit
His grandmother had given him for his trip to France.
At the restaurant after they ordered he felt sick and left for the loo.
He dropped his trousers and squatted on his heels over the hole.

No one heard him shouting because the loo was in a separate building.
His pal finally came to find him after half an hour.
Since it was Sunday no one could buy him new pants in a store.
No one among the restaurant staff had an extra pair.

White linen summer clouds squatted over Điện Biên Phủ.
It must be 1954 because you soil yourself and give up hope but don't.
The boys are reading *L'Étranger* as summer reading.
My country, 'tis of thee, Albert Camus!

The host sprinted upstairs to grab his fellow Existentialist—
To drag him downstairs to the Embassy's July Fourth garden party.
The Ambassador's son died horribly the following year
In a ski lodge fire.

GRANDSON BORN DEAD

The baby born dead
Better lie down.
Better stand up.
Better get up and go out
For a walk.
He stands around in the rain
In the room.
Breathe two three four.
And down in the rain in the drain
In the floor.
Babies born dead
Drown in the main in the more.
Better a walk.
The head on a stalk
Laughs and waves.
It is the sun with its rays.
The sun wants to talk.
If you start to be sick,
If you start to be stuck,
If you have to sit down,
If one foot starts to drop,
If hope starts to stop,
You will drown
In the drain in the main in the more.
The rain is downtown.
Up here is happy.

Get up!
Get up, get out of bed!
Wake up!
Wake up, you sleepyhead!
All right. Go ahead.
Be dead.

DEATH

Dapper in hats,
Dapper in spats,
Espousing white tie and tails or a tailcoat and striped trousers
With dancing-backward Ginger Rogers and other espousers,

Singing with such sweet insincere
Dated charm and good cheer,
And his toupee of slicked-down dated hair;
Immortal date-stamped Fred Astaire!

EAST HAMPTON AIRPORT

East Hampton Airport is my shepherd.
It was smaller when I took lessons.
The shepherd's crook has high-tech runway lights now.
The shack became a terminal.
The private jets drop by to sleep.
I stand in the afternoon in the open field across the road.
The light planes come in low.
The dog doesn't even look up.
Their wings wave around frantically
Through the valley of the shadow of death.
They touch down calmly and taxi to a stop.

East Hampton Airport is my harbor.
I shall not want.
The harbormaster maketh me to lie down
In green pastures he has paved over.
He leadeth me beside the runway's still waters.
He keeps me in the air so I can land.
I stand in the open field on the far side of Wainscott Road
And watch the summer, autumn, winter sky.
It was my idea to take up flying,
To die doing something safer than motorcycling.
I went up with my instructor not to learn, just to fly.

I stand in the field opposite the airport.
I watch the planes flying in and the planes flying out.
My proud Irish terrier takes pills for his cardiomyopathy.
Before we bark our last,
Our hearts enlarge and burst.
George Plimpton went to bed
And woke up dead.
I write this poem thinking of the painter David Salle
Who wants to make a movie
About the poet Frank O'Hara.
A beach taxi on Fire Island hit Frank and he burst, roll credits.

I remember flying back from Montauk.
I was flying the plane.
The instructor asked me, "Notice anything?"
Yes. The plane was absolutely stuck—
Speechless—ecstatically still.
The headwinds were holding us in place in space.
We were flying, but not moving, visibility forever.
The ocean was down there waving.
The engine purred contentment.
I am flying, but not moving.
I stand in a field and stare at the air.

A WHITE TIGER

The golden light is white.
It is the color of moonlight in the middle of the night
If you suddenly wake and you are a child
In the forest and the wild
Animals all around you are sleeping.
You are in your bed and you are weeping
For no reason.
It is because it is tiger season.
The big-game hunters' guns are banging.
The corpse of a real beauty is hanging
From a tree in the darkness, waiting.
Of *course*, the Palestinians and the Jews are exaggerating!
The building is not a million stories high.
The moonlight is not going to die.
The Israelis and the Palestinians are by no means exaggerating.
The carcass is hanging from the darkness, waiting.
The building is a million human stories high.
The moonlight is going to die.
In the corners of your little room,
The large-bore guns go *boom boom*.
The tigers are field dressed where they fall, who used to roar.
The stomach and lungs are removed with the gore.
Tiger incisors get sold at the store.
Tiger canines ground into powder get sold at the store.

Tiger heart will also restore.
The tigers will end up a tiger skin on the floor.
Especially a rare white tiger is not safe anywhere anymore.
One escaped from the cage when they opened the door.

Rest in fierce peace, Edward, on the far shore.

CLOCLO

The golden person curled up on my doormat,
Using her mink coat as a blanket,
Blondly asleep, a smile on her face, was my houseguest
The Goat who couldn't get her set of keys to work, so blithely
Bedded down to wait in the apartment outside hall.
A natural animal elegance physically
Released a winged ethereal exuberance,
Pulling g's, then weightlessness, the charm of the divine,
Luxuriously asleep in front of the front door like a dog.
Dear polymorphous goddess who past sixty
Could still instantly climb a tree,
But couldn't get the metal key
To turn in any residence
In London or New York or Calabria or Greece or Florence.
Always climbing anything (why
Someone had dubbed her The Goat when she was young),
Climbing everywhere in a conversation,
Up the Nile, up the World Trade Center Twin Towers,
Upbeat, up late, up at dawn, up for anything,
Up the ladder to the bells.
A goat saint lived ravishingly on a rock,
Surrounded by light, dressed in a simple frock,
The last great puritan aesthete
In the Cyclades.
She painted away
Above the Greek blue sea.

She chatted away
Beneath the Greek blue sky.
Every year returned to London.
So European. So Jamesian.
Every year went back
To Florence, her first home.
To the thirty-foot-high stone room in Bellosguardo.
To paint in the pearl light the stone gave off.
Ten generations after Leonardo had painted on the same property.
She worked hard as a nun
On her nude landscapes of the south,
With their occasional patio or dovecote and even green bits,
But never people or doves, basking in the sun.
Believed only in art.
Believed in tête-à-têtes.
Believed in walks to the top of the hill.
Knew all the simple people, and was loved.
It comes through the telephone
From Florence when I call that she has died quietly a minute ago,
Like a tear falling in a field of snow,
Climbing up the ladder to the bells out of Alzheimer's total whiteout,
Heavenly Clotilde Peploe called by us all Cloclo.

LAUDATIO

A young aristocrat and Jew and German
The rise of Hitler sent to school in London.
St. Paul's School made a man a gentleman.
The gentleman grew up to be a boy.

The boy came to America to become a dashing OSS officer.
The boy slipped into Germany to meet the schoolboys plotting to
        kill Hitler.
The boy became a not bad postwar racecar driver.
The boy became a heterosexual clothes designer.

A Jewish boy donned the uniform of an SS officer,
Cross-dressing across Deathland in the final months of the war,
Urbane inside his skull-and-crossbones attire—
The first John Weitz fashion show, my dear!

When Weitz wanted to obliterate his SS tattoo,
He burned it off with a cigarette just like the real SS.
The underground network he would infiltrate had removed theirs.
A mysterious beautiful woman was involved. It gets better.

There is the story of how he needed publicity
For his fashion line and couldn't spend much money.
No one had thought of putting advertisements on the back
Of New York City buses back then.

Weitz wrote koans for the age of Warhol.
I don't understand John Weitz advertising
Went rolling down Fifth Avenue behind a bus.
He looked like a distinguished diplomat when he ate a wurst.

Weitz had the lofty friendliness of a duke.
He was full of goy.
He was not discreet.
He admired the great.

He could operate on automatic pilot
With his beautiful manners.
He had unreal good looks.
He used his mellifluous voice.

John Weitz belonged to clubs, loved boats,
Told lovely anecdotes, bad jokes, wrote cordial biographies
Of colorless Third Reich personalities.
He loved honors and he loved glory.

He kept the Iron Cross
Of his father from the First World War framed on the wall.
He denied that he was dying.
He never sighed until the moment after he died.

TO DIE FOR

The ants on the kitchen counter stampede toward ecstasy.
The finger chases them down while the herd runs this way and that way.
They are alive while they are alive in their little way.
They burst through their little ant outfits, which tear apart rather easily.

The little black specks were shipped to Brazil in ships.
The Portuguese whipped the little black specks to bits.
The sugar plantations on the horrible tropical coast where the soil was rich
Were a most productive ant Auschwitz.

The sugar bowl on the counter is a D-cup, containing one large white
        breast.
The breast in the bowl is covered by excited specks
That are so beyond, and running around, they are wrecks.
They like things that are sweet. That's what they like to eat.

The day outside is blue and good.
God is in the neighborhood.
The nearby ocean puts liquid lure in each trap in the set of six,
Paving the way to the new world with salt and sweet.

They sell them at the hardware store on Main Street.
Inside each trap is a tray that gives them a little to eat
And sends them back.
There is light in Africa, and it is black.

I was looking for something to try for.
I was looking for someone to cry for.
I was looking for something to die for.
There isn't.

BARBADOS

Literally the most expensive hotel in the world
Is the smell of rain about to fall.
It does the opposite, a grove of lemon trees.
I isn't anything.
It is the hooks of rain
Hovering with their sweets inches off the ground.
I is the spiders marching through the air.
The lines dangle the bait
The ground will bite.
Your wife is as white as vinegar, pure aristo privilege.
The excellent smell of rain before it falls overpowers
The last aristocrats on earth before the asteroid.
I sense your disdain, darling.
I share it.

The most expensive hotel in the world
Is the slave ship unloading Africans on the moon.
They wear the opposite of space suits floating off the dock
To a sugar mill on a hilltop.
They float into the machinery.
The machine inside the windmill isn't vegetarian.
A "lopper" lops off a limb caught
In the rollers and the machine never has to stop.
A black arm turns into brown sugar,
And the screaming rest of the slave keeps the other.
His African screams can't be heard above the roar.
A spaceship near the end of a voyage was becalmed.
Two astronauts floated weightlessly off the deck
Overboard into the equator in their chains and *splash* and drowned.

A cane toad came up to them.
They'd never seen anything so remarkable.
Now they could see the field was full of them.
Suddenly the field is filled with ancestors.
The hippopotamuses became friendly with the villagers.
Along came white hunters who shot the friendly hippos dead.
If they had known that friendship would end like that,
They never would have entered into it.
Suddenly the field is filled with souls.
The field of sugarcane is filled with hippopotamus cane toads.
They always complained
Our xylophones were too loud.
The Crocodile King is dead.
The world has no end.

The crocodile explodes out of the water and screams at the crowd
That one of them has stolen his mobile phone.
On the banks of the muddy Waddo, *ooga-booga!*
What about a Christmas tree in a steamy lobby on the Gulf of Guinea!
Because in Africa there are Africans
And they are Africans and are in charge.
Even obstipation
Can't stop a mighty nation.
The tragic magic makes lightning.
Some of the young captives are unspeakable
In their beauty, and their urine makes lightning, black and gold.
The heat is so hot
It will boil you in a pot.
Diarrhea in a condom is the outcome.

The former president completely loses it and screams from the stage
That someone fucking stole his fucking phone.
The audience of party faithful is terrified and giggles.
This was their man who brought the crime rate down
By executing everyone.
The crocodile staged a coup
And ended up in prison himself
And then became the president.
He stood for quality of life and clitorectomy.
But in his second term, in order to secure those international loans,
The crocodile changed his spots to free speech.
Lightning sentences them at birth to life without parole
With no time off for good behavior.
At that point in the voyage the ocean turns deeper.

People actually suffered severe optical damage from the blinding effects
Of the white roads in full sunlight.
It is the island roads so white you can't see,
Made of crushed limestone snow.
It is the tropical rain the color of grapefruit
Hovering in the figure of the goddess Niscah
Above the tile roof of the plantation house.
She dangles her baited lines.
It is the black of the orchids in a vase.
The goddess overpowers the uprising
And *I* is the first one hacked to pieces.
The asteroid is coming to the local cinema.
It is a moonlit night with the smell of rain in the air.
Thump thump, speed bump.

The most expensive hotel in the world ignites
As many orgasms as there are virgins in paradise.
These epileptic foaming fits dehydrate one,
But justify the cost of a honeymoon.
The Caribbean is room temperature,
Rippling over sand as rich as cream.
The beach chair has the thighs of a convertible with the top down.
You wave a paddle and the boy
Runs to take your order.
Many things are still done barefoot.
Others have the breakout colors of a parrot.
In paradise it never rains, but smells as if it could.
Two who could catapulted themselves overboard into the equator.
I die of thirst and drown in chains, in love.

Into the coconut grove they go. *Into the coconut grove they go.*
The car in the parking lot is theirs. *The car in the parking lot is theirs.*
The groves of lemon trees give light. *Ooga-booga!*
The hotel sheds light. *Ooga-booga!*
The long pink-shell sky of meaning wanted it to be, but really,
The precious thing is that they voted. *Ooga-booga!* And there we were,
The cane toads and the smell of rain about to fall.
The crocodiles and spiders are
The hippos and their friends who shot them dead.
The xylophone is playing too loud
Under the coconut palms, which go to the end of the world.
The slave is screaming too loud and we
Can't help hearing
Our tribal chant and getting up to dance under the mushroom cloud.

CLIMBING EVEREST

The young keep getting younger, but the old keep getting younger.
But this young woman is young. We kiss.
It's almost incest when it gets to this.
This is the consensual, national, metrosexual hunger-for-younger.

I'm getting young.
I'm totally into strapping on the belt of dynamite
Which will turn me into light.
God is great! I suck Her tongue.

I mean—my sunbursts, and there are cloudbursts.
My dynamite penis
Is totally into Venus.
My penis in Venus hungers and thirsts,

It burns and drowns.
My dynamite penis
Is into Venus.
The Atlantic off Sagaponack is freezing black today and frowns.

I enter the jellyfish folds
Of floating fire.
The mania in her labia can inspire
Extraordinary phenomena and really does cure colds.

It holds the Tower of Pisa above the freezing black waves.
The mania is why
I mention I am easily old enough to die,
And actually it's the mania that saves

The Tower from falling over.
Climbing Everest is the miracle—which leaves the descent
And reporting to the world from an oxygen tent
In a soft pasture of cows and clover.

Happening girls parade around my hospice bed.
The tented canopy means I am in the Rue de Seine in Paris.
It will embarrass
Me in Paris to be dead.

It's Polonius embarrassed behind the arras,
And the arras turning red.
Hamlet has outed Polonius and Sir Edmund Hillary will wed
Ophelia in Paris.

Give me Everest or give me death.
Give me altitude with an attitude.
But I am naked and nude.
I am constantly out of breath.

A naked woman my age is just a total nightmare,
But right now one is coming through the door
With a mop, to mop up the cow flops on the floor.
She kisses the train wreck in the tent and combs his white hair.

ORGANIZED RELIGION

Will you? Everything? Anything? Weird stuff, too?
I want to do anything you want me to.
I will meet you in an hour in the mirror.
I will meet you in front of the mirror.

When the cars have their lights on in the daytime when it's raining,
And the full-length bedroom mirror is the hostess entertaining,
And the summer downpour thrillingly thrashes the windows,
My naked in high heels shows me she can touch her toes!

The rainy city outside stretches around the world.
The rainy season inside the mirror gets whirled
Into a waterspout. No doubt
The dolphins in the mirror know what water is about!

You love it all.
I love it when you make me get down on all fours and crawl.
I put you on a leash and spank you.
I thank you.

The value of life which will end is unbearable,
And these are just some ways of bearing it. The joy is terrible.
The joy is actually terrible.
The sweetness of life is actually unbearable.

God looks up to His creation by dint of lying on the floor.
God lies there on His back on the carpet and looks. That's what you
    are for.
Hike your skirt up higher. There is nothing higher or more
Than Him you stand over and adore!

MOTHER NATURE

Mother Nature walked from Kenya.
Going faster is Italian.
Going fast got you nowhere.
Madagascar is impatiens.

Came the warriors of the nations,
Came the Delawares and Mohawks,
Came the Choctaws and Comanches,
Came the Mandans and Dacotahs,

Came the Hurons and Ojibways,
All the warriors drawn together
By the signal of the peace pipe.
And they stood there on the meadow,

With their weapons and their war gear,
Painted like the leaves of autumn,
Painted like the sky of morning,
Wildly glaring at each other.

The smiling Indian economy is running uphill inputting,
Outrunning a rising ocean of sweat.
The poor stay behind and drown
In their own brown.

Technology is the placenta
Feeding the fetus dreams.
It was high tide.
It was wet dreams.

Skira reproduced the paintings,
Mother Nature at Ajanta,
Her beauty, her big breasts,
Her athleticism, her shoreline, her high tides.

The orbit was Aryan.
Sanskrit debris floats by a boy in orbit in St. Louis.
Anything to see those breasts
In that art book!

By the shore of Gitche Gumee,
By the shining Big-Sea-Water,
Hiawatha liked the white man,
Liked Caucasians, liked their smell.

From the waterfall he named her,
Laughing Water, Minnehaha.
Mother Nature, you, my mother,
Help the paleface ask me for my colored hand in marriage!

And the great chief liked his odor,
And he offered him his daughter,
Redskin jewel from a giant, legend waiting for an answer,
And the frightened white man could not answer.

Mother Nature went to China,
China the vagina.
Wet dreams conceive there,
Where no one wants a daughter.

I pin the throttle on the straight
Toward China all night,
With the moon out and the stars,
And reach Kabul.

The nightclub bombing in Bali
Shattered Baghdad.
The hotel temple dancers hold the sky up.
The elephant lifts his friend the tiger to safety.

The satellite picks up a faint signal
From the Arabian Peninsula
From long before Islam
Of the immortal Imru' al-Qays declaiming his ode.

Whalesong surfaces in the desert and spouts.
The Arab Pindar pinpricks the emptiness.
A nanosecond of moisture
Irrigates ancient Arabia.

His she-camel is a Ferrari with a saddle
Who knows the desert by heart and is unafraid.
He praises her in his monorhymes of tribal twaddle
About this and that and the brevity of life.

The Prophet Muhammad
Acknowledged his fame
As the finest poet in hell
Where the pre-Islamic poets dwell.

Let shuttered windows shatter
To let the bomb-blast in.
Everyone is screaming.
The exits have been padlocked.

Everyone is screaming.
Muhammad took away their silliness.
Muhammad is the firestorm.
Everyone converts.

Her breast is bigger than I am.
Her nipple is bigger than my mouth.
Let me masturbate to death.
Let my hand fall off.

Islam is submission.
Behead the man
Who will not listen!
My head and hand are coming to an end.

I am coming in Manhattan
By the shining Big-Sea-Water.
I am coming to the end. I am coming to.
The predawn streets are empty.

This is what it feels like.
Everyone is screaming.
I am coming, Mother Nature.
I am coming, Mannahatta.

I am coming in Manhattan.
This is what it comes to.
Everyone is screaming. All the planes are grounded.
The exits have been padlocked.

The asteroid is really coming.
The president in Washington is speaking to the world.
The sea tilts up and down
Next to the silent dawn.

BROADWAY MELODY

A naked woman my age is a total nightmare.
A woman my age naked is a nightmare.
It doesn't matter. One doesn't care.
One doesn't say it out loud because it's rare
For anyone to be willing to say it,
Because it's the equivalent of buying billboard space to display it,

Display how horrible life after death is,
How horrible to draw your last breath is,
When you go on living.
I hate the old couples on their walkers giving
Off odors of love, and in City Diner eating a ray
Of hope, and then paying and trembling back out on Broadway,

Drumming and dancing, chanting something nearly unbearable,
Spreading their wings in order to be more beautiful and more terrible.

LOVE SONG

I shaved my legs a second time,
Lagoon approaching the sublime,
To cast a moonlight spell on you.
TriBeCa was Tahiti, too.

I know I never was on time.
I was downloading the sublime
To cast a moonlight spell on you.
TriBeCa was Tahiti, too.

The melanoma on my skin
Resumes what's wrong with me within.
My outside is my active twin.
Disease I'm repetitious in.

The sun gives life but it destroys.
It burns the skin of girls and boys.
I cover up to block the day.
I also do so when it's gray.

The sunlight doesn't go away.
It causes cancer while they play.
Precancerous will turn out bad.
I had an ice pick for a dad.

A womanizing father, he's
The first life-threatening disease.
His narcissistic daughter tried
To be his daughter but he died.

The richest man in Delaware
Died steeplechasing, debonair.
One company of ours made napalm.
That womanizing ice pick's gray calm

Died steeplechasing in a chair,
The jockey underneath the mare.
She posted and she posted and
Quite suddenly he tried to stand

And had a heart attack and died,
The ice pick jockey's final ride.
The heart attack had not been planned.
He saw my eyes and tried to stand.

My satin skin becomes the coffin
The taxidermist got it off in.
He stuffed me, made me lifelike. Fatten
My corpse in satin in Manhattan!

My body was flash-frozen. God,
I am a person who is odd.
I am the ocean and the air.
I'm acting out. I cut my hair.

You like the way I do things, neat
Combined with craziness and heat.
My ninety-eight point six degrees,
Warehousing decades of deep freeze,

Can burst out curls and then refreeze
And have to go to bed but please
Don't cure me. Sickness is my me.
My terror was you'd set me free.

My shrink admired you. He could see.
Sex got me buzzing like a bee
With Parkinson's! Catastrophe
Had slaughtered flowers on the tree.

My paranoia was revived.
I love it downtown and survived.
I loved downtown till the attack.
Love Heimliched me and brought me back.

You brought me life, glued pollen on
My sunblock. Happy days are gone
Again. My credit cards drip honey.
The tabloids dubbed me "Maid of Money."

Front-page divorce is such a bore.
I loathed the drama they adore.
You didn't love me for my money.
You made the stormy days seem sunny.

BREAST CANCER

The intubated shall be extubated and it rains green
Into the uptown air because it is almost raining.
You can smell the sidewalks straining.
The side streets are contagious but serene.
The disease is nutritious.
The bitter medicine delicious.
The beautiful breasts are repetitious.
The much older man you love is vicious.

The man will be even older by the time
She takes down the book to read the poem.

RILKE

As he approaches each tree goes on,
And the girls one by one
Glance down at their blouses. A nun,
Then six or seven, hop in
A cream station wagon,
White-beaked blackbirds baked in a pie.
In his mind is
The lid of an eye
The dark dilated closing behind him.

Rilke. Arched eyebrows and shadowed
Moist eyes. An El Greco. Swart, slim.
He's late to her. He thinks of her, waiting,
Limb by limb.

Her defenselessness and childlike trust!
Smiling to be combed out
And parted—and her lust
Touching the comb like a lyre.
To have been told by her not to trust her!

And he distrusts her.

And everywhere he sees
Hunchbacks and addicts and sadists
In braces in the cities,

Roosting in their filth,
Or plucking the trees,
In New York for true love,
In Boston for constancy.
You can be needed by someone
Or needy, thinks Rilke.

They clutch their loves like addicts
Embracing when they see
Hot May put out her flowers.
Or clutch themselves. They can't shake free.

He thinks of the time
He lived by her calendar
When she missed her time.

She gave the child a name.

When she bled, she laughed and gasped
Tears warm as pablum
On his wrists. But that is past.

Rilke feels his body
Moving in front of his last
Step. He sweats, and thinks
Of the rubble massed
On Creusa behind Aeneas's
White-hot shoulders and neck.

Addresses
And clothesline laundry swelled
Like pseudocyesis—
That's what he has to pass through.

His tie is her blue,
And a new lotion gives him an air
Of coolness. He combs his hair,
And tries to smooth his hair.

He'll be there,
The husband. She'll have left him asleep—
A nap, beyond the top stair,
In darkness.

Light, light is in the trees
Pizzicato, and mica
Sizzles up to his knees.
A dozen traffic lights
Swallow and freeze
And one by one relay red red
Like runners with a blank message.

I hate her, I hate her, he said
A minute ago. Curls cluster
Rilke's dark head.

CASANOVA GETTING OLDER

Do they think they are being original when they say
This is a new thing for me to ask, and ask
Do you love me?
Everyone these days keeps asking
Do you love me?
Everyone says
This is a new thing for me to ask.
The answer is yes.
This is a new thing for me to ask.

The answer is yes I don't.
Do you love me?
The answer is yes.
The eyes glisten with feeling.
The creature hath a purpose and its eyes are bright with it.
This sudden pecking of asking, of being asked, is this.
The answer is yes I don't.
The heart got the shot but got the flu anyway,
And the body aches, and fever and chills, and can't sleep.

The forest shivers with fever.
Their mother pulls their covers up.
The whippoorwill keeps calling *whippoorwill whippoorwill.*
Do you love me? Do you love me? I don't love you.
Not everyone is afraid.
Not everyone feels vulnerable.
Everyone is afraid of the terrible joy. I do.
Each other is Mecca,
The hajj to the Other.

IL DUCE

More than one woman at a time
Is the policy that got the trains running on time.
More than one at a time in those fascist days, and I climb
Into the clouds and then above—the sublime!—
And wag my wings and make it rhyme.

More than one woman at a time was enough.
On time because there were enough.
Mussolini in riding boots stood at his desk to stuff
Himself into the new secretary who was spread out on the desk. He goes *uff.*
He goes *uff wuff, uff wuff,* and even—briefly—falls in luff.

It's getting worse, and I don't like the way it sounds.
Down in the subway, while you are waiting, all those humming sounds.
In New York City, all the Lost-and-Founds.
All the towed-away-car pounds.
While you are waiting on the subway platform—God's wounds! Zounds!

Mussolini is standing on the little balcony
Above Italy, and Italy is looking up at Mussolini on the balcony,
Who is looking over at Ethiopia across a deep blue sea.
I never have enough for me.
I am getting on a girl motorcycle to go across the sea to see.

I AM SIAM

I saw the moon in the sky at sunset over a river pink as a ham.
I am the governess imported from England by me,
The widowed King of Siam.
I drop down on one knee.
I want to marry me.
Where you are I am.
Là où tu es je suis. Où tu es je suis.
I drop down on one knee.
I want to marry me.
I do a *saut de chat* at sunset over a silver spoon of jam.
Jam for the royal children, Felicity
And Sam.
I am the English governess imported from England by me.
I am the widowed King of Siam! The widowed King of Siam!

THE BIG JET

The big jet screamed and was hysterical and begged to take off,
But the brakes held it in place to force it to flower.
The runway was too short, that's why, kiddo.
Till the engines powered up to full power.

In a little school in what was then still called Burma, not yet cancered,
Carolyn was teaching English to the lovely brownish children.
The assignment was to use the word "often" in a sentence.
"Birds fly more often than airplanes," the boy answered.

Little sudden flowers in the desert after it rains,
Bearing gifts of frankincense and myrrh . . .
What thou lovest well remains.
Birds fly more often than airplanes.

Meat-eating seagulls shout their little cries *myanmar myanmar* above the
    airport,
Dropping razor clams on the runway to break them open.
Hard is soft inside.
The big jet has soft people inside for the ride.

THE BLACK-EYED VIRGINS

A terrorist rides the rails underwater
From one language to another in a packed train of London
Rugby fans on their way to the big match in Paris
And a flock of Japanese schoolgirls ready to be fucked
In their school uniforms in paradise.
This is all just after Madrid in the reign of terror.
This is the girls' first trip outside Japan.
The terrorist swings in the hammock of their small skirts and black socks.
The chunnel train stops in the tunnel with an announcement
That everyone now alive is already human remains.
The terrorists have seen to it that trains
Swap human body parts around with bombs.
The Japanese schoolgirls say so sorry.
Their new pubic hair is made of light.

EUROSTAR

Japanese schoolgirls in their school uniforms with their school
    chaperones
Ride underwater on a train
Every terrorist in the world would dearly love to bomb
For the publicity and to drown everybody.
The Eurostar dashes into the waves.
The other passengers are watching the Japanese girls eat
Little sweeties they bought with their own money
In London. President Bush the younger is making ice cream.
Ice cream for dessert
Is what Iraq is, without the courses that normally come before.
You eat dessert to start and then you have dessert.
One of them is a Balthus in her short school skirt standing on the seat.
She reaches up too high to get something out of her bag.
She turns around smiling because she knows where you are looking.

SONG: "THE SWOLLEN RIVER OVERTHROWS ITS BANKS"

The terrorists are out of breath with success.
And cancer is eating American women's breasts.
The terrorists are bombing Madrid
And everywhere serious and nice.
They put the backpacks on
Without a word and leave
The Italian Premier talking to an empty room because
They leave the TV on and leave.
One of the many networks Mr. Berlusconi owns
Carries him live denouncing terror. The man
By now has reached Milan
Who has the man in London for Miami.
Both will board the train,
As in the swollen river overthrows its banks.

DRINKING IN THE DAYTIME

Anything is better than this
Bliss.
Nursing on a long-stemmed bubble made of crystal.
I'm sucking on the barrel of a crystal pistol
To get a bullet to my brain.
I'm gobbling a breast, drinking myself down the drain.

I'm in such a state of Haut-Brion I can't resist.
A fist-fucking anus swallowing a fist.
You're wondering why I talk this way, so daintily!
I'll tell you after I take a pee.
Now I'm back.
Oilcoholics love the breast they attack.

I'm talking about the way poetry made me free.
It's treated me very well, you see.
I climbed up inside the Statue of Liberty
In the days when you could still go up in the torch, and that was me.
I mean every part I play.
I'm drinking my lunch at Montrachet.

I'm a case of Haut-Brion turning into tar.
I'm talking about the recent war.
It's a case of having to raise your hand in life to be
Recognized so you can ask your question. *Mr. Secretary! Mr. Secretary!*
To the Secretary of Defense, I say:
I lift my tar to you at Montrachet!

I lift my lamp beside the golden door to pee,
And make a vow to make men free, and we will find their WMD.
Sir, I supported the war.
I believe in who we are.
I dedicate red wine to that today.
At Montrachet, near the Franklin Street stop, on West Broadway.

THE BUSH ADMINISTRATION

I

The darkness coming from the mouth
Must be the entrance to a cave.
The heart of darkness took another form
And inside is the Congo in the man.
I think the Bush Administration is as crazy as Sparta was.
Sparta has swallowed Congo and is famished.
The steel Spartan abs turn to fevered slush
While it digests the good that it is doing
In the desert heat. I felt a drop of rain,
Which is the next Ice Age being born.

II

I stood on Madison. The sun was shining.
I felt large drops of rain as warm as tears.
I held my hand out, palm up, the way one does.
The sun was shining and the rain really started.
Maybe there must have been a rainbow somewhere.
I hailed a cab and as I hopped in
That was the first thing
The radio said:
They had beheaded an American.
There was a thunderclap and it poured.

III

The downpour drumming on my taxi gets the Hutu in me dancing.
Il rombo della Desmosedici makes machete music.
I crawl into a crocodile
And I go native.
The white cannibals in cowboy boots
Return to the bush
And the darkness of the brutes.
I am on all fours eating grass
So I can throw up because I like the feeling.
I crouch over a carcass and practice my eating.

IV

The United States of America preemptively eats the world.
The doctrine of eat lest you be eaten
Is famished, roars
And tears their heads off before its own is sawed off.
The human being sawing screams *God is Great!*
God is—and pours cicadas
By the tens of millions through the air.
They have risen from underground.
The voices of the risen make a summer sound.
It is pouring cicadas on Madison Avenue, making the street thick.

V

Every human being who has ever lived has died,
Except the living. The sun is shining and
The countless generations rise from underground this afternoon
And fall like rain.
I never thought that I would see your face again.
The savage wore a necklace made of beads,
And then I saw the beads were tiny human faces talking.
He started crying and the tears were raindrops.
The raindrops were more faces.
Everybody dies, but they come back as salt and water.

VI

I am charmed by my taxi's sunny yellow reflection
Keeping abreast of the speeding taxi I'm in,
Playful and happy as a dolphin,
All the way down York Avenue to the hospital,
Right up to the bank of elevators to heaven.
I take an elevator to the floor.
Outside the picture window, rain is falling on the sunshine.
In the squeeze-hush silence, the ventilator keeps breathing.
A special ops comes in to check the hoses and the flow.
A visitor holds out his palm to taste the radiant rain.

VII

The Bush Administration likes its rain sunny-side up.
I feel a mania of happiness at being alive
As I write you this suicide note.
I have never been so cheerily suicidal, so sui-Seidel.
I am too cheery to be well.
George Bush is cheery as well.
I am cheeriest
Crawling around on all fours eating gentle grass
And pretending I am eating broken glass.
Then I throw up the pasture.

VIII

CENTCOM is drawing up war plans.
They will drop snow on Congo.
It will melt without leaving a trace, at great expense.
America will pay any price to whiten darkness.
My fellow citizen cicadas rise to the tops of the vanished Twin Towers
And float back down white as ashes
To introduce a new Ice Age.
The countless generations rise from underground this afternoon
And fall like rain.
I never thought that I would live to see the towers fall again.

THE DEATH OF THE SHAH

Here I am, not a practical man,
But clear-eyed in my contact lenses,
Following no doubt a slightly different line than the others,
Seeking sexual pleasure above all else,
Despairing of art and of life,
Seeking protection from death by seeking it
On a racebike, finding release and belief on two wheels,
Having read a book or two,
Having eaten well,
Having traveled not everywhere in sixty-seven years but far,
Up the Eiffel Tower and the Leaning Tower of Pisa
And the World Trade Center Twin Towers
Before they fell,
Mexico City, Kuala Lumpur, Accra,
Tokyo, Berlin, Teheran under the Shah,
Cairo, Bombay, L.A., London,
Into the jungles and the deserts and the cities on the rivers
Scouting locations for the movie,
A blue-eyed white man with brown hair,
Here I am, a worldly man,
Looking around the room.

Any foal in the kingdom
The Shah of Iran wanted
He had brought to him in a military helicopter
To the palace.
This one was the daughter of one of his ministers, all legs, a goddess.
She waited in a room.
It was in the afternoon.

I remember mounds of caviar before dinner
In a magnificent torchlit tent,
An old woman's beautiful house, a princess,
Three footmen for every guest,
And a man who pretended to get falling-down drunk
And began denouncing the Shah,
And everyone knew was a spy for the Shah.

A team of New York doctors (mine among them)
Was flown to Mexico City to consult.
They were not allowed to examine the Shah.
They could ask him how he felt.

The future of psychoanalysis
Is a psychology of surface.
Stay on the outside side.
My poor analyst
Suffered a stroke and became a needy child.
As to the inner life: let the maid.

How pathetic is a king who died of cancer
Rushing back after all these years to consult more doctors.
Escaped from the urn of his ashes in his pajamas.
Except in Islam you are buried in your body.
The Shah mounts the foal.
It is an honor.
He is in and out in a minute.
She later became my friend
And married a Texan.

I hurry to the gallery on the last day of the show
To a line stretching around the block in the rain—
For the Shah of sculptors, sculpture's virile king,
And his cold-rolled steel heartless tons.
The blunt magnificence stuns.
Cruelty has a huge following.
The cold-rolled steel mounts the foal.

The future of psychoanalysis is it has none.

I carry a swagger stick.
I eat a chocolate.
I eat brown blood.

When we drove with our driver on the highways of Ghana
To see for ourselves what the slave trade was,
Elmina was Auschwitz.
The slaves from the bush were marched to the coast
And warehoused in dungeons under St. George's Castle,
Then FedExed to their new jobs far away.

One hotel kept a racehorse as a pet.
The owner allowed it the run of the property.
Very shy, it walked standoffishly
Among the hotel guests on the walkways and under the palms.
The Shah had returned as a racehorse dropping mounds of caviar
Between a coconut grove and the Gulf of Guinea.

An English royal is taught to strut
With his hands clasped behind his back.
A racehorse in West Africa kept as a pet
Struts the same way the useless royals do,
Nodding occasionally to indicate he is listening.
His coat has been curried until he is glistening.

Would you rather be a horse without a halter
Than one winning races being whipped?
The finish line is at the starting gate, at St. George's Castle.
The starting gate is at the finish line for the eternal life.
God rears and whinnies and gives a little wave.
He would rather be an owner than a slave.

Someone fancy says
How marvelous money is.
Here I am, an admirer of Mahatma Gandhi,
Ready to praise making pots of money
And own a slave.
I am looking in the mirror as I shave the slave.
I shave the Shah.
I walk into the evening and start being charming.

A counterfeiter prints me.
(The counterfeiter *is* me.)
He prints Mohammad Reza Shah Pahlavi.

I call him Nancy.
He is so fancy.
It is alarming
He is so charming.
It is the thing he does and knows.
It is the fragrance of a rose.
It is the nostrils of his nose.
It is the poetry and prose.
It is the poetry.
It is a horse cab ride through Central Park when it snows.
It is Jackie Kennedy's hairpiece that came loose,
That a large Secret Service agent helped reattach.

I remember the Duck and Duckess of Windsor.
You could entertain them in your house.

Here I am, looking around the room
At everyone getting old except the young,
Discovering that I am lacking in vanity,
Not that I care, being debonair,
Delighted by an impairment of feeling
That keeps everything away,
People standing around in a display case
Even when they are in bed with you,
And laser-guided bombs destroy the buildings
Inside the TV, not that I care,
Not that I do not like it all,
Not that I am short or tall,
Not that I do not like to be alive,
And I appeal to you for pity,
Having in mind that you will read this
Under circumstances I cannot imagine
A thousand years from now.

Have pity on a girl, perdurable, playful,
And delicate as a foal, dutiful, available,
Who is waiting on a bed in a room in the afternoon for God.
His Majesty is on his way, who long ago has died.
She is a victim in the kingdom, and is proud.
Have pity on me a thousand years from now when we meet.
Open the mummy case of this text respectfully.
You find no one inside.

Printed in the USA
CPSIA information can be obtained
at www.ICGtesting.com
LVHW091147150724
785511LV00005B/591